Level

2

Vocabulary Enrichment Workbook

Santillana USA
www.santillanausa.com

ISBN: 1-58986-526-X

Santillana USA Publishing Company, Inc.
2105 N.W. 86th Avenue
Miami, FL 33122

Printed in the United States of America

10 09 08 07 06   10 11 12 13 14 15

Our mission is to make learning and teaching English and Spanish
an experience that is motivating, enriching, and effective for both
teachers and students. Our goal is to satisfy the diverse needs of our
customers. By involving authors, editors, teachers and students, we
produce innovative and pedagogically sound materials that make
use of the latest technological advances. We help to develop
people's creativity. We bring ideas and imagination into education.

TO THE TEACHER

Welcome to the *Vocabulary Enrichment Workbook*

The goal of the *Vocabulary Enrichment Workbook* is to reinforce the concepts, vocabulary, and language structures taught in Santillana Intensive English (SIE). The activities in the *Vocabulary Enrichment Workbook* are extensions from the lessons taught in SIE.

Each level of SIE is divided into 12 thematic units. Each unit contains ten lessons. Each lesson is printed on a Lesson Card. To teach each lesson, the teachers simply follow the lesson plan on the Lesson Card. Each card uses a clear three-step approach: Teach, Practice/Apply, and Extend. Included at the bottom right-hand corner of each Lesson Card are the instructions for each activity in the *Vocabulary Enrichment Workbook*. When finished, the *Vocabulary Enrichment Workbook* will serve as a permanent record of student achievement and may be incorporated into assessment portfolios.

The *Vocabulary Enrichment Workbook* tasks should be assigned after completing each SIE lesson card. They should be corrected and returned to students. This procedure may be modified in situations when students are at different stages of language acquisition in the same classroom. Following are brief descriptions of the stages of language acquisition (see Stephen D. Krashen, *The Natural Approach: Language Acquisition in the Classroom*, Upper Saddle River, NJ: Prentice Hall, 1996).

Stage 1, Preproduction
Learners have minimal or no comprehension of English. They may participate in activities by saying *yes* or *no* or by using gestures.

Stage 2, Early Production
Learners have some comprehension of English. They participate in activities by responding with single words or short phrases in English.

Stage 3, Speech Emergence
Learners participate in activities by responding with longer phrases and complete sentences. They engage in conversation, narrate events, and express opinions.

Stage 4, Intermediate Fluency
Learners use a wide variety of topics in conversation, speak extemporaneously, and can interpret shades of meaning.

The following chart compares the *Vocabulary Enrichment Workbook* tasks with learners at the four stages of language acquisition. The filled-in boxes indicate learners at different stages of language acquisition and the tasks they are able to complete.

		TASKS				
STAGES OF LANGUAGE ACQUISITION		filling in the blank	labeling	matching	writing sentence	drawing	writing paragraph
	Preproduction						
	Early Production						
	Speech Emergence						
	Intermediate Fluency						

The tasks that are most challenging for Preproduction and Early Production learners are writing sentences and paragraphs. Students at those stages can still participate in these writing activities if some oral preparation is done in class and they work in pairs with students at a higher stage of language acquisition. Oral preparation might include a discussion of the subject, writing the key words on the board for students to copy and learn, and providing oral and written examples. The lower-level learner might begin by copying the correct work of a more proficient partner but should be encouraged to produce original writing as well. As the academic year progresses, less pair work should be necessary. If more proficient students are not available to work with the lower-level students, adult or student tutors or the classroom teacher may be asked to work with them.

For your convenience, each activity gives, at the bottom of the page, the ESL progress indicator based on the TESOL (Teachers of English to Speakers of Other Languages) ESL standards. Following is a list of the ESL Indicators.

ESL INDICATORS

The Teachers of English to Speakers of Other Languages (TESOL) organization has established goals for ESOL learners at all grade levels. Each goal is associated with three standards:

Goal 1: Use English to communicate in social settings.

Standards for Goal 1:

1. Use English to participate in social interaction.
2. Interact in, through, and with spoken and written English for personal expression and enjoyment.
3. Use learning strategies to extend their communicative competence.

Goal 2: Use English to achieve academically in all content areas.

Standards for Goal 2:

1. Use English to interact in the classroom.
2. Use English to obtain, process, construct, and provide subject matter information in spoken and written form.
3. Use appropriate learning strategies to construct and apply academic knowledge.

Goal 3: Use English in socially and culturally appropriate ways.

Standards for Goal 3:

1. Use the appropriate language variety, register, and genre according to audience, purpose, and setting.
2. Use nonverbal communication appropriate to audience, purpose, and setting.
3. Use appropriate learning strategies to extend their sociolinguistic and sociocultural competence.

Sample Progress Indicators are provided as assessable, observable activities for students to perform and show progress in meeting each standard.

The Santillana Intensive English (SIE) Program has included in each lesson card the goals and standards covered. In addition, the *Vocabulary Enrichment Workbooks* will show at the end of each page the progress indicator which will be accomplished through the completion of each activity.

Dr. Arnhilda Badía
Educational Research Consultant

Name

Name

Lupita

Carlos

Maylee

Nicolas

Pao

Sara

Name

1

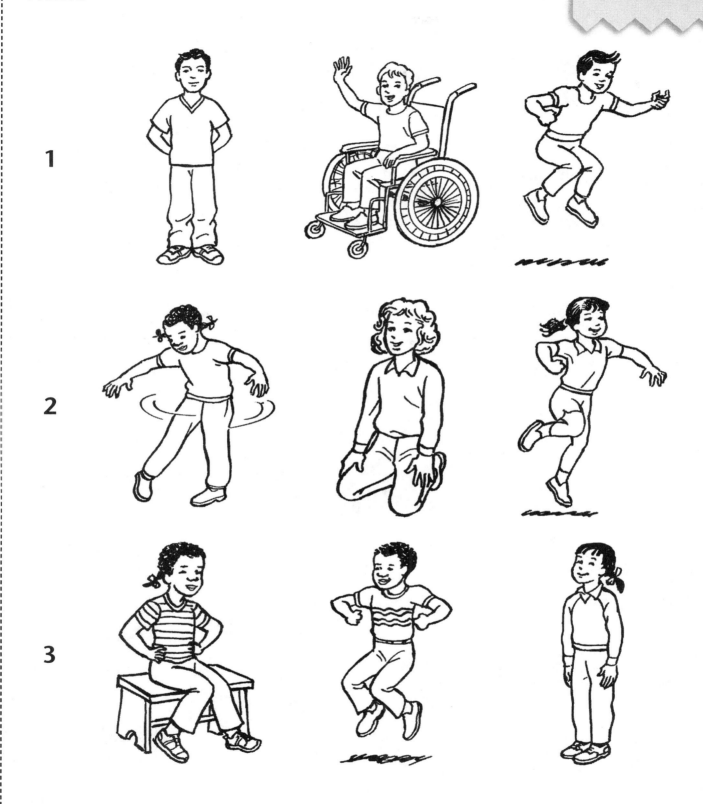

2

3

Name

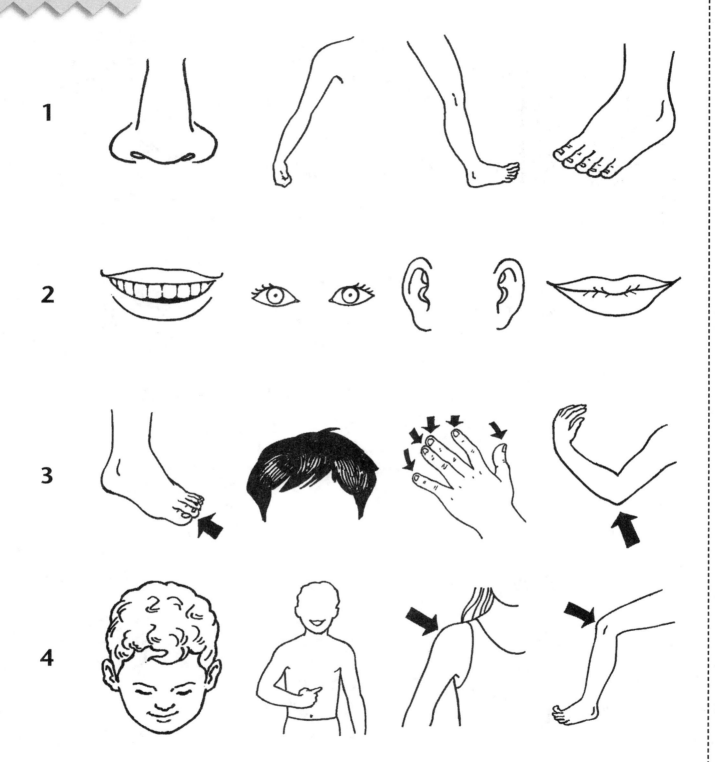

1

2

3

4

Name

Name

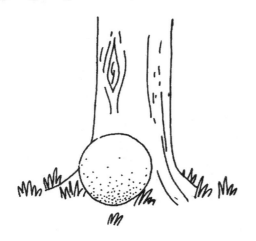

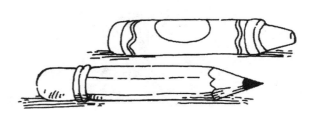

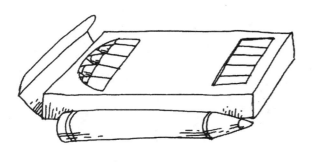

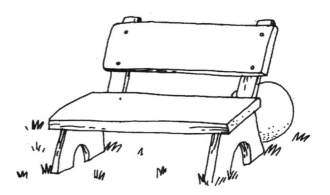

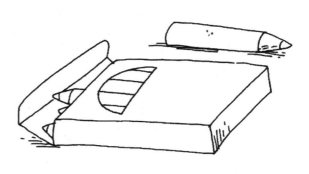

Name

1

2

3

2.10

Name

walk   bus   bike   car

Name

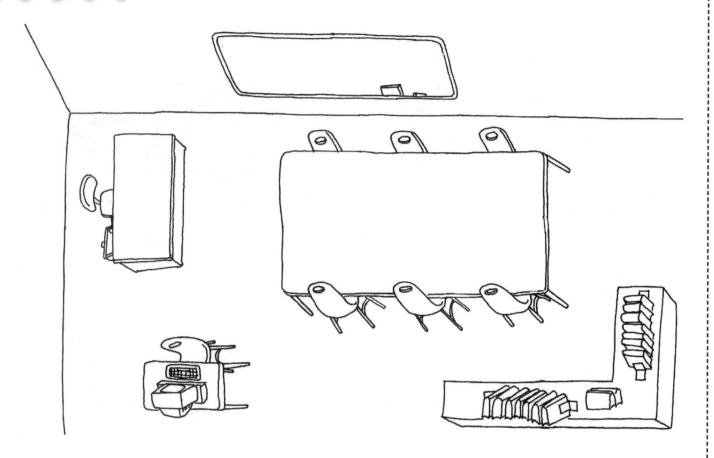

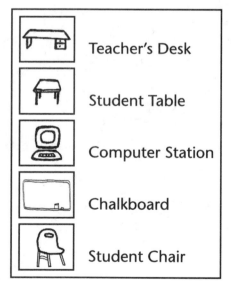

Teacher's Desk	
Student Table	
Computer Station	
Chalkboard	
Student Chair	

1. Where is the teacher's desk?

2. Where is the computer?

3. Where is the chalkboard?

4. Where is the student table?

5. How many chairs are at the student table?

calendar

glue stick

book

pen

pencil

ruler

computer disk

pencil sharpener

scissors

crayon

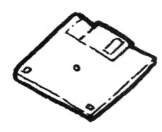
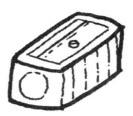

Goal 1, Standard 1/ESL Indicator: Identify and associate objects presented through pictures with written words.

Name

Name

| monkey | snake | moon |
| sandwich | map | sweater |

1

_____

2

_____

3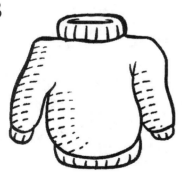

_____

4

_____

5

_____

6

_____

 Circle all the words that begin with the "M" sound. Then color all the words that begin with the "S" sound.

Goal 2, Standard 2/ESL Indicator: Recognize beginning letter sounds.

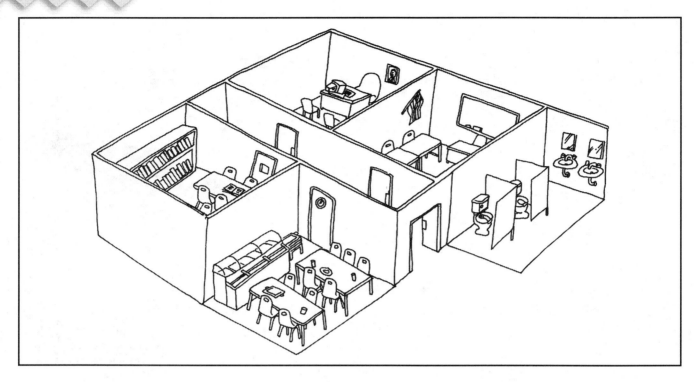

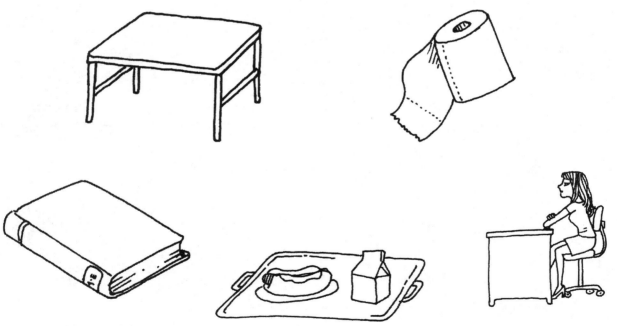

Name

My School Cafeteria

Name

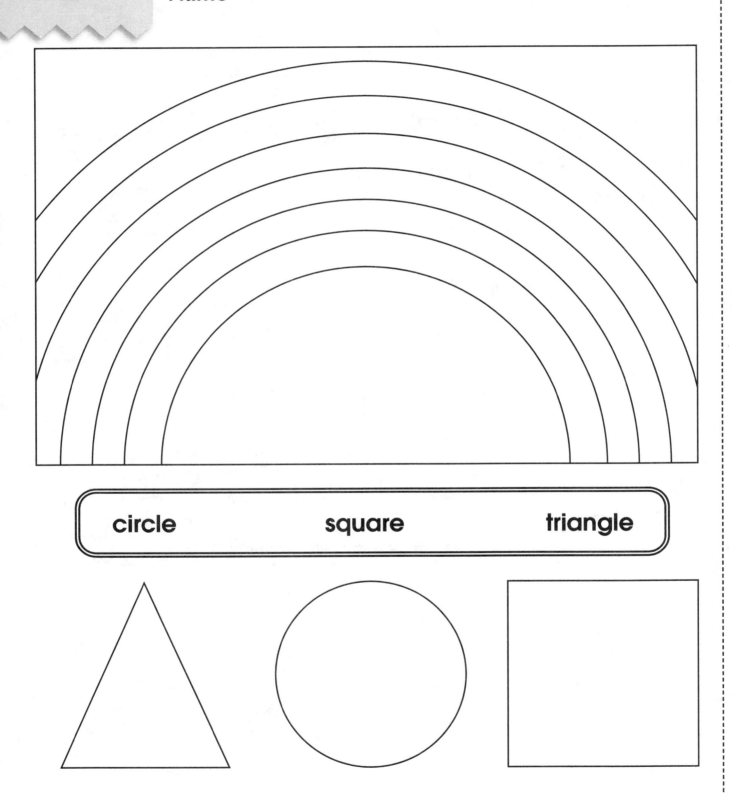

circle   square   triangle

funny　　　　**fish**

A _____ can swim.

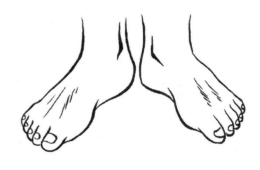

father　　　　**feet**

I walk on my _____.

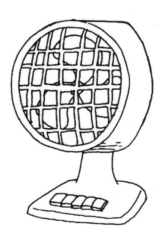

fork　　　　**feet**

I eat with a _____.

family　　　　**fan**

A _____ keeps me cool.

| gate | game | grapes |
| guitar | goose | goat |

_____   _____   _____

  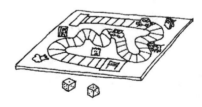

_____   _____   _____

Mom	Dad	Sisters	Brothers

1. How many people are in this family? _____

2. How many brothers are in this family? _____

3. How many sisters are in this family? _____

4. How many children are in this family? _____

5. This family has six _____.

6. This family has four _____.

Goal 3, Standard 3/ESL Indicator: Analyze a graph to respond to questions related to family members.

Name

| tall | taller | tallest |

Name

| father | mother | sister | brother | baby |

1

The one in the circle is the _____.

2

The one in the circle is the _____.

3

The one in the circle is the _____.

Goal 2, Standard 2/ESL Indicator: Complete sentences with appropriate words based on an illustration.

Name

1	jog	grapes	jelly	log
2	jam	pet	jet	see
3	mouse	home	hold	house
4	man	fan	fork	my
5	dog	sun	play	fun
6	boy	girl	toy	get
7	hot	ham	jam	jet
8	bus	call	bee	tree

Goal 2, Standard 2/ESL Indicator: Identify rhyming words to demonstrate phonemic awareness.

Name _____

2.27

mobile home	apartment	house	houseboat

1

I would like to live in a

_____

3

I would like to live in a

_____

2

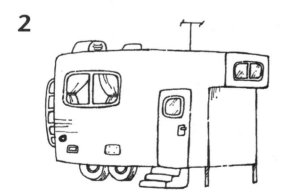

I would like to live in a

_____

4

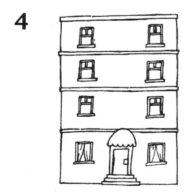

I would like to live in an

_____

 Circle your favorite home to live in.

Goal 1, Standard 1/ESL Indicator: Identify different living facilities and show preferences.

Name _____

letter   stamp   address

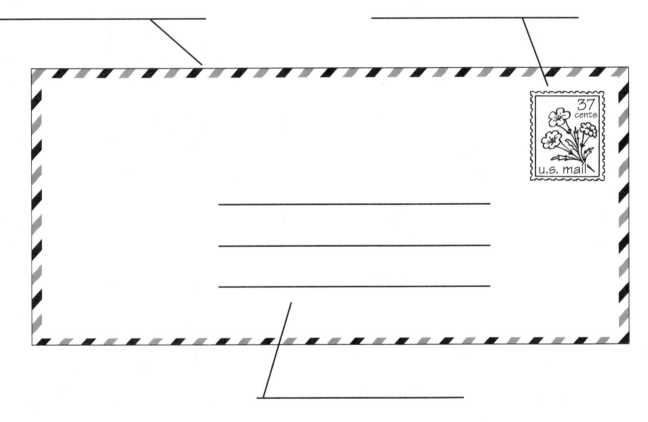

_____   _____

_____

_____

_____

_____

1. A _____ goes on the top, right hand corner of

a letter.

2. I will write the _____ on the letter.

3. You need a stamp to mail a _____ .

 Complete the sentences with the words in the box.

Sara

Lupita

Maylee

Jason

Nicolas

1. At night, I put on my pajamas and go to sleep.

2. In the morning, I eat breakfast.

3. In the evening, our family eats dinner.

4. In the afternoon, I eat lunch at school.

Look at each picture and determine the time of day by orally stating if it is morning, afternoon, or evening.

Name

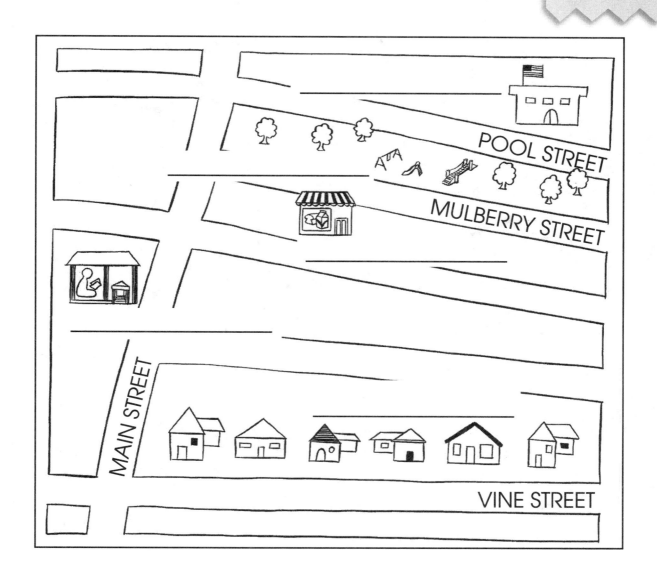

Pao's house

Library

Park

School

Grocery store

Goal 1, Standard 1 / ESL Indicator: Clarify and restate information based on an illustration.

Name

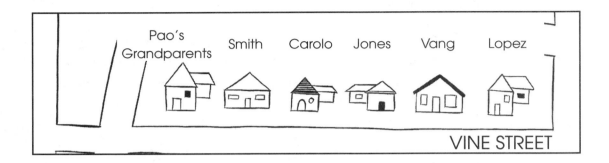

Pao's Grandparents   Smith   Carolo   Jones   Vang   Lopez

VINE STREET

1. Pao's grandparents live on Vine Street.

2. There are 4 houses on Vine Street.

3. The Jones' house is next to the Vang's house.

 Circle the word that goes with the picture.

lake snake

bee tree

man fan

park dark

Goal 1, Standard 3/ESL Indicator: Associate illustrations with written labels to demonstrate word recognition.

first　　　　second　　　　third

_____

_____

_____

Goal 2, Standard 2/ESL Indicator: Represent an appropriate sequence of illustrations related to plant growth.

| zebra | nest | pencil | queen |

1

_____ _____ _____ _____

| quilt | pig | necklace | zipper |

2

_____ _____ _____ _____

| net | pin | quarter | zoo |

3

_____ _____ _____ _____

EXTENSION ACTIVITY Color all the words that have the beginning sound of "Z"–red, "P"–blue, "Q"–yellow and "N"–green.

Goal 2, Standard 2/ESL Indicator: Name the beginning letter sound of words to demonstrate phonemic awareness.

long a

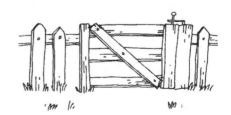

Name

Goal 2, Standard 2 /ESL Indicator: Compare and classify objects according to characteristics.

smaller   bigger

The dog is _____.

The doll is _____.

The bike is _____.

The box is _____.

The cake is _____.

The horse is _____.

Name

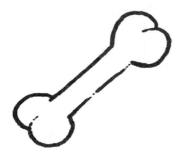

bowl

rose

nose

bone

doll

boat

coat

mop

Goal 1, Standard 3/ESL Indicator: Associate illustrations with written labels to demonstrate word recognition.

Name

cub	**cube**

1. I would like an ice _____.

tube	**tub**

2. Toothpaste comes in a _____.

mud	**mule**

3. A _____ is an animal.

blue	**block**

4. The sky is _____.

Name

apartment	cow	bus

1

_____   _____   _____

skyscraper	sheep	bridge

2

_____   _____   _____

parade	zoo	barn

3

_____   _____   _____

Goal 2, Standard 1/ESL Indicator: Compare and classify objects to determine which ones belong to a particular setting.

Name _____

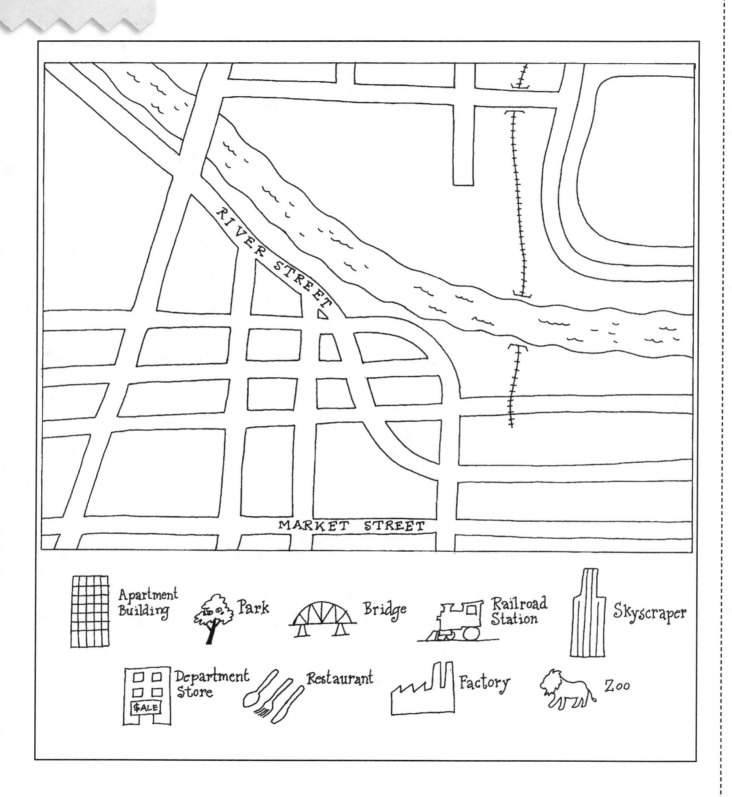

Apartment Building   Park   Bridge   Railroad Station   Skyscraper

Department Store   Restaurant   Factory   Zoo

Goal 1, Standard 3/ESL Indicator: Follow verbal directions to find information on charts or maps.

MARKET STREET

BROADWAY

 Zoo

 Railroad Station

Apartment Building

1. The apartment building is on _____ Street.

2. The railroad station is on _____.

3. The zoo is on the corner of _____ Street

and _____.

 Circle the pictures with the long "a" sound.

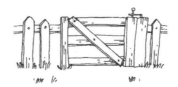

Goal 2, Standard 2/ESL Indicator: Recognize pictures and identify words with specific vowel sounds to demonstrate phonemic awareness.

Draw a line to all pictures that have a short "O" vowel sound.

short o

Goal 2, Standard 2/ESL Indicator: Recognize short vowel sounds of words presented through pictures to demonstrate phonemic awareness.

Name _____

   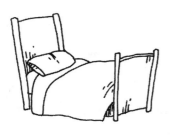

Goal 2, Standard 2/ESL Indicator: Recognize pictures and identify words with specific vowel sounds to demonstrate phonemic awareness.

Name

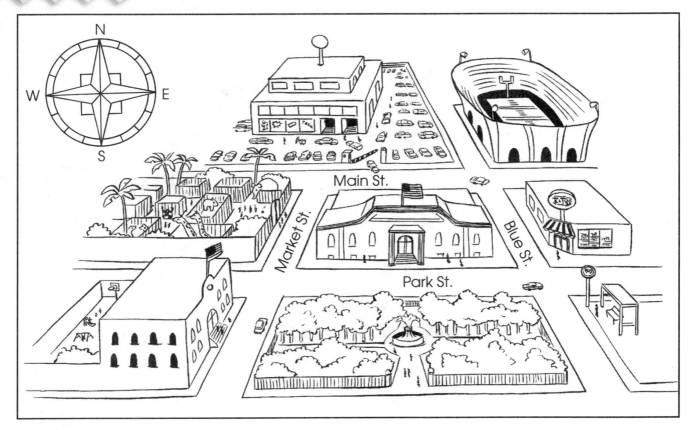

1. From the bus stop the bus goes west on Park Street.

2. Then, the bus turns right on Market Street.

3. The bus passes the City Zoo and goes right on Main Street.

4. You get off the bus at the corner of Main Street and Blue Street.

5. What building do you see to the North?

_____

Goal 2, Standard 2/ESL Indicator: Use information from a map or chart to construct meaning.

Name

__ iger

__ ebra

__ iraffe

__ izard

__ ippopotamus

__ strich

Goal 2, Standard 2/ESL Indicator: Identify and associate illustrations with written symbols to construct meaning.

Name

Goal 2, Standard 1/ESL Indicator: Recognize pictures and identify words with specific vowel sounds to demonstrate phonemic awareness.

walk __ __ __

1. She is _____ with us.

pick __ __ __

2. I am _____ flowers for my mother.

do __ __ __

3. What are you _____?

park __ __ __

4. My dad is _____ the car.

work __ __ __

5. Is he _____ at the grocery store?

play __ __ __

6. We will be _____ soccer today.

roast __ __ __

7. The machine is _____ the peanuts.

fill __ __ __

8. The worker is _____ the jars with peanut butter.

Goal 2, Standard 2/ESL Indicator: Show appropriate use of new vocabulary, phrases, and structures in writing.

Name

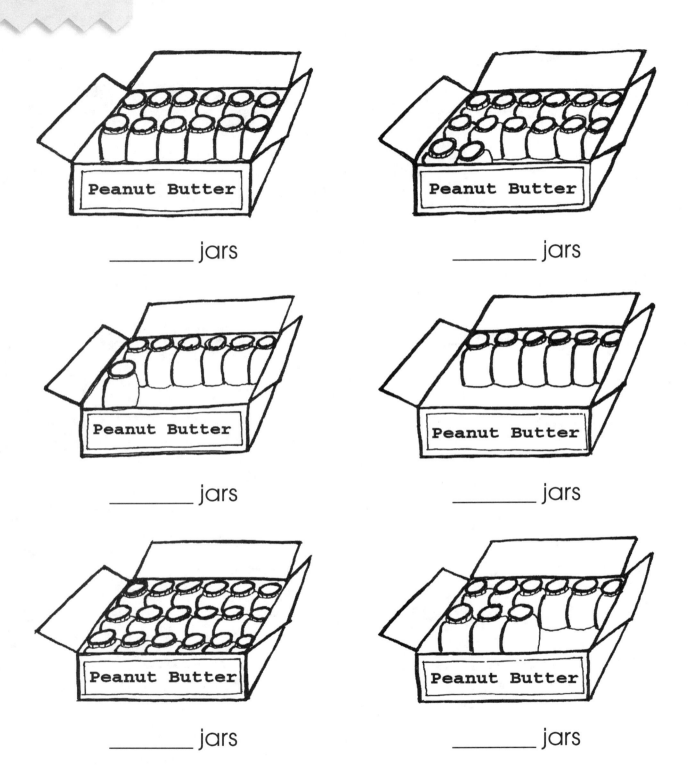

_____ jars

_____ jars

_____ jars

_____ jars

_____ jars

_____ jars

Name

| Stop | Yield | One Way | School Crossing |

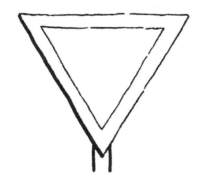

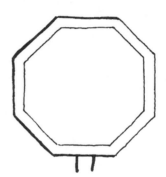

_____

_____

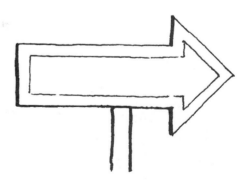

_____

_____

Name

Station 3 Schedule		
Going To:	**Leaves:**	**Arrives:**
Bear Valley Mall	9:30 A.M.	9:50 A.M.
City Library	9:35 A.M.	9:45 A.M.
East Beach	9:50 A.M.	10:00 A.M.
Blue Street Park	9:55 A.M.	10:20 A.M.
City Hall	11:55 A.M.	12:10 P.M.
Bee Shoe Factory	1:10 P.M.	1:20 P.M.
Main Street Shops	2:30 P.M.	2:50 P.M.
Main Street Bus Station	3:10 P.M.	3:25 P.M.
Lions' Stadium	4:20 P.M.	4:55 P.M.
City Zoo	5:35 P.M.	6:00 P.M.

1. The bus to City Hall leaves Station 3 at _____.

2. The last bus to leave Station 3 is going to _____.

3. The bus to City Library arrives at _____.

4. The bus after the City Hall bus is the _____ bus.

5. If you want to go to East Beach, you will leave Station

   3 at _____.

Goal 1, Standard 3/ESL Indicator: Interpret information presented in a chart or graph to determine different bus schedules.

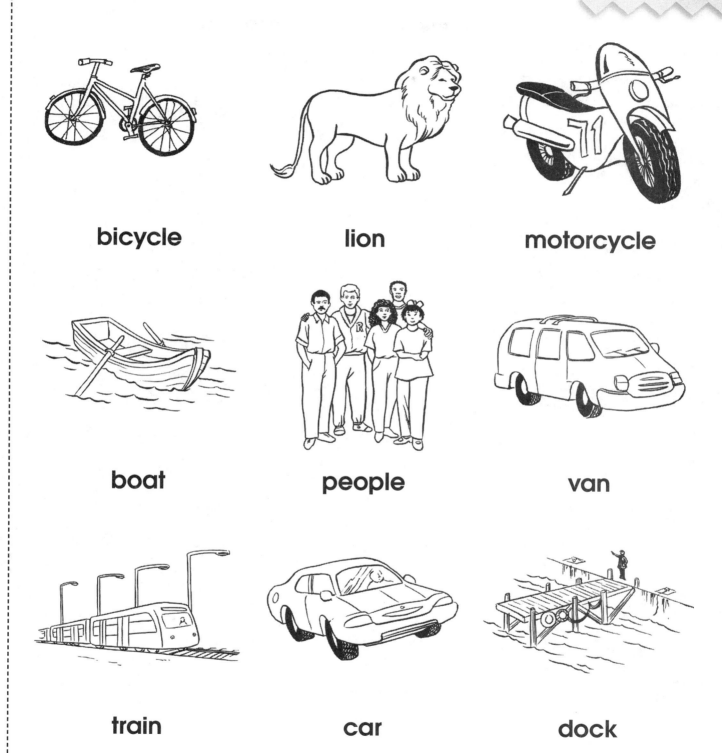

bicycle

lion

motorcycle

boat

people

van

train

car

dock

Goal 2, Standard 2/ESL Indicator: Compare and classify objects according to functions or characteristics.

Name

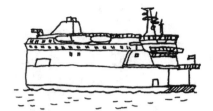

Depart	Arrive	Number of Hours
New York, NY 8:30 A.M.	Boston, MA 9:30 A.M.	
San Diego, CA 8:45 A.M.	Sacramento, CA 9:45 A.M.	
Dallas, TX 9:00 A.M.	Chicago, IL 11:45 A.M.	
Miami, FL 1:00 P.M.	Atlanta, GA 2:10 P.M.	
Memphis, TN 3:05 P.M.	Tulsa, OK 4:00 P.M.	
Washington, DC 4:20 P.M.	Newark, NJ 5:10 P.M.	
Baltimore, MD 6:00 P.M.	Orlando, FL 8:25 P.M.	

earlier　　　later

 is _____ than

 is _____ than

 is _____ than

is _____ than

Name

fast   faster   fastest

Name

| trolley | taxi | bicycle |
| milk wagon | bus | train |

_____

_____

_____

_____

_____

_____

Circle the kinds of transportation that are still used today.

Goal 2, Standard 2 /ESL Indicator: Compare and contrast objects to determine time relationships.

Name

Travel in the Past

Travel Today

Travel in the Future

spaceship _____

milk wagon _____

car _____

Circle the beginning letter sound and underline the ending letter sound of each transportation word.

cans

bottles

trash

paper

 Circle the begining sound of each vocabulary word.

Goal 2, Standard 2/ESL Indicator: Recognize and write beginning letter sounds to demonstrate phonemic awareness.

Name _____

Week	1	2	3	4	5	6	7	8	9	10
Jones	1	1	2	1	2	2	2	1	1	2
Hong	2	1	1	1	3	2	3	1	1	1
Rodriguez	2	1	2	2	2	2	2	2	2	2
Sanchez	3	3	1	1	1	1	1	1	2	1
Green	1	2	2	2	3	2	1	1	3	2

The families on our block recycle. For 10 weeks we all counted the number of recycling containers we filled.

1. How many recycling containers did the Hong family fill in the 10 weeks? __16__

2. How many recycling containers did the Sanchez family fill in the 10 weeks? __15__

3. How many recycling containers did all the families fill in the first week? __9__

4. How many recycling containers did the Jones family fill in the 10 weeks? __15__

5. How many recycling containers did all the families fill in the third week? __8__

Goal 2, Standard 3/ESL Indicator: Analyze information presented in a chart to construct meaning.

> clean   recycle   neighborhood

1. We _____ cans in our neighborhood.

2. Recycling helps keep our lawn _____.

3. We like our _____ to be clean.

 Match the words with their abbreviations.

Monday	Tues.
Tuesday	Sat.
Wednesday	Thurs.
Thursday	Mon.
Friday	Sun.
Saturday	Wed.
Sunday	Fri.

Name

1. maylee and her family recycle plastic

Maylee and her family recycle plastico

2. saras family recycles paper plastic and glass

Saras family recycles paper, plastic, and glass.

3. does your family recycle plastic or glass

Does your family recyle plastic or glass?

4. my familys recycling can is blue

My family's recycling can are blue.

5. carlos put 25 glass jars in his familys recycling can

Carlos put 25 jars in his familysrecycling cans.

6. did carlos find more glass jars than maylee

Did Carlos find more glass jars than Maylee?

Name

Lupita and Pao have been collecting cans and bottles. They want to take them to the recycling center. They will get 3¢ for each can and 5¢ for each bottle.

1. If Lupita has 8 cans, how much money will she get from the recycling center?

$3 + 3 + 3 + 3 + 3 + 3 + 3 + 3 =$ ___24___ ¢

$8 \times 3 =$ ___24___ ¢

2. If Pao has 5 cans and 2 bottles, how much money will he get from the recycling center?

$3 + 3 + 3 + 3 + 3 =$ ___15___ ¢

$5 \times 3 =$ ___15___ ¢

$5 + 5 =$ ___10___ ¢

$2 \times 5 =$ ___10___ ¢

___15___ ¢ for cans plus ___10___ ¢ for bottles = ___25___ ¢

3. How much money did they get together?

Lupita got ___60___ ¢.

Pao got ___15___ ¢.

Together they got ___25___ ¢.

Name

hammer	saw	screwdriver
hoe	hose	ax

1. Use a _____ to put a nail into a board.

2. Use an _____ to cut down a small tree.

3. Use a _____ to get earth ready for seeds.

4. Use a _____ to cut a board into two pieces.

5. Use a _____ to water your garden.

6. A _____ will turn a screw.

Name

plant seeds	rake leaves
water flowers	shovel snow

_____

_____

_____

_____

did not

1. Sara _____ want to go with me.

can not

2. I _____ find my cat.

would not

3. Mother _____ want me to go there.

could not

4. I _____ go out to play with my friends.

was not

5. My sister _____ the only one who lost a ticket.

is not

6. It _____ time to go to the party.

had not

7. Pao _____ been at school all week.

Goal 1, Standard 3/ESL Indicator: Practice recently-learned vocabulary by completing sentences with words provided.

Name

> doctor   blacksmith   dressmaker
> baker   teacher   sheriff

1. The _____ helped sick neighbors.

2. The _____ put shoes on horses.

3. The _____ helped children read.

4. The _____ baked bread.

5. The _____ helped keep people safe.

6. The _____ sewed clothes.

Goal 2, Standard 3/ESL Indicator: Identify and associate pictures with written labels to complete sentences.

police officer

teacher

- This worker grows our food.

- This worker helps us learn.

doctor

- This worker keeps us safe.

- This worker keeps us healthy.

truck driver

- This worker brings us our food.

farmer

Goal 2, Standard 2/ESL Indicator: Associate pictures with sentences that describe functions.

Name

baker   newspaper worker
firefighter   ambulance driver

_____ _____ _____ _____

 Make corrections on the sentences by putting in capitals and ending punctuation.

1. joe works at the bakery to bake bread at night

2. the newspaper prints the paper at night

3. saras mother drives an ambulance at night

4. my brother is a firefighter who works at night

Goal 2, Standard 1/ESL Indicator: Edit written assignments to demonstrate knowledge of punctuation and capitalization.

Name

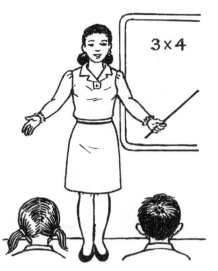

_____

_____

_____

_____

_____

_____

Goal 2, Standard 2/ESL Indicator: Identify and associate professions with time schedules as presented through illustrations.

Name

boots   helmet   air mask   hose   air tank

1. Firefighters use a _____ to protect their heads.

2. The _____ protect the firefighter's feet.

3. The _____ and _____ help firefighters

   breathe.

4. The firefighter uses a _____ to spray water on

   the fire.

Goal 1, Standard 3/ESL Indicator: Associate illustrations with written words to construct meaning.

> this   that   these

1. Does the firefighter wear boots?

   Yes, _____ are his boots.

2. Does the baker wear an apron?

   Yes, _____ is her apron.

3. Does the police officer wear a badge?

   Yes, _____ is her badge.

Goal 1, Standard 3/ESL Indicator: Associate illustrations with written information to construct meaning.

Name

1. Sara wants to buy two 37-cent stamps.
   How much will she spend?

   $2 \times 37 =$ _____

2. Carlos needs three 37-cent stamps.
   How much will he spend?

   $3 \times 37 =$ _____

3. Pao needs one 37-cent stamp and one 10-cent stamp.
   How much will he spend?

   $37 + 10 =$ _____

Complete the chart. Fill in the number of letters that each person got. The first one is done for you.

	1	2	3	4	5	6
Pao 2	▨	▨				
Sara 4						
Carlos 3						
Maylee 5						
Lupita 1						
Jason 5						
Nicolas 6						

Goal 2, Standard 2/ESL Indicator: Construct a chart or other graphic device with the information provided.

The painter paints the walls.

_____

The workers pour the foundation.

_____

The carpenters build the walls.

_____

Goal 2, Standard 2/ESL Indicator: Recognize a sequence followed to complete a task.

computer   **uses**

1. My father _____ a _____ at work.

works   **office**

2. My sister _____ in an _____.

shops   **mall**

3. Maylee _____ at the _____.

house   **like**

4. I _____ Pao's blue _____.

runs   **sister**

5. Carlos _____ as fast as his _____.

school   **take**

6. Will you _____ me to _____?

rug   **walks**

7. The cat _____ on the _____.

jacket	jackets

bees	bee

dress	dresses

bug	bugs

rugs	rug

bike	bikes

rug   **rugs**

1. We have two _____ in our house.

bee   **bees**

2. A _____ was on the flower.

jacket   **jackets**

3. She wants to wear that _____ .

bug   **bugs**

4. There is a _____ on my arm.

Goal 1, Standard 3/ESL Indicator: Show appropriate use of new vocabulary, phrases, and structures by completing sentences with the correct word.

farm

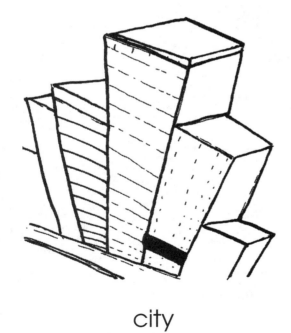

city

orange grove

orchard

apartment

bus

pig

farmer

park

duck

skyscraper

☐

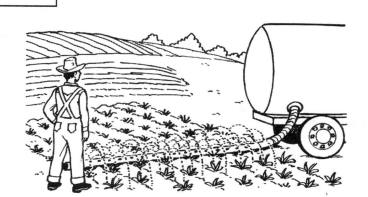

1. The planter puts seeds in the ground.

☐

2. The corn goes to a processing plant.

☐

3. The farmer waters the plants.

Goal 2, Standard 2/ESL Indicator: Explain changes in plant growth based on an illustration and written information.

is   **are**

1. My sister _____ in the first grade.

is   **are**

2. There _____ bees in the garden.

is   **are**

3. We _____ going to the park today.

is   **are**

4. July _____ a hot month.

is   **are**

5. Maylee _____ as tall as Sara.

is   **are**

6. He _____ going to school.

is   **are**

7. The cats _____ sleeping on the rug.

Goal 1, Standard 3/ESL Indicator: Show appropriate use of new vocabulary, phrases, and structures by completing sentences with the correct word.

First   Second   Third

_____ , you spread the peanut butter on your bread.

_____ , you get some bread to make your sandwich.

_____ , you eat your sandwich.

Goal 2, Standard 2/ESL Indicator: Determine a sequence of events based on illustrations.

2.86

Name

first	second	third

Goal 2, Standard 2/ESL Indicator: Describe in writing a sequence of events based on illustrations.

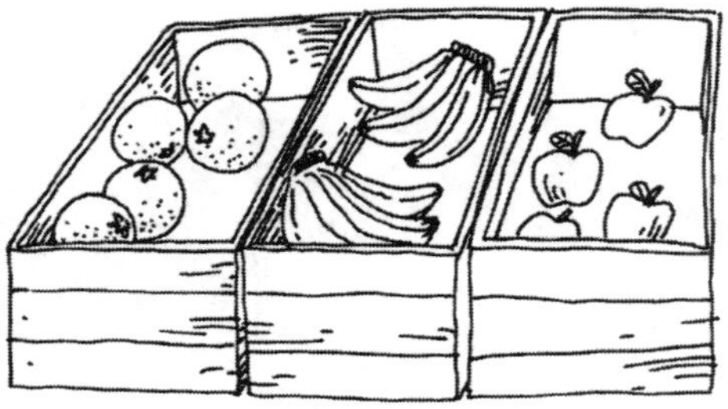

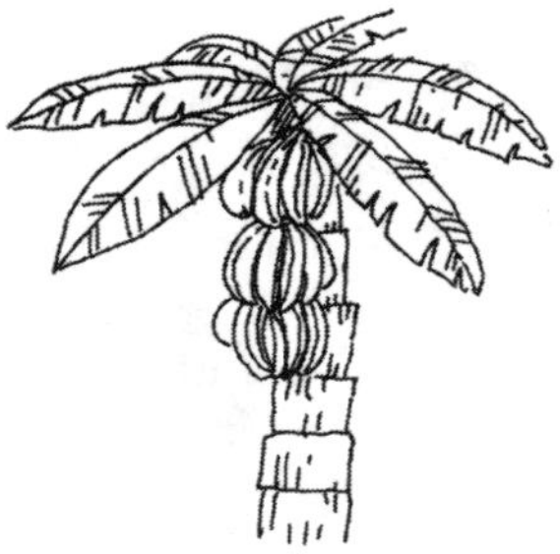

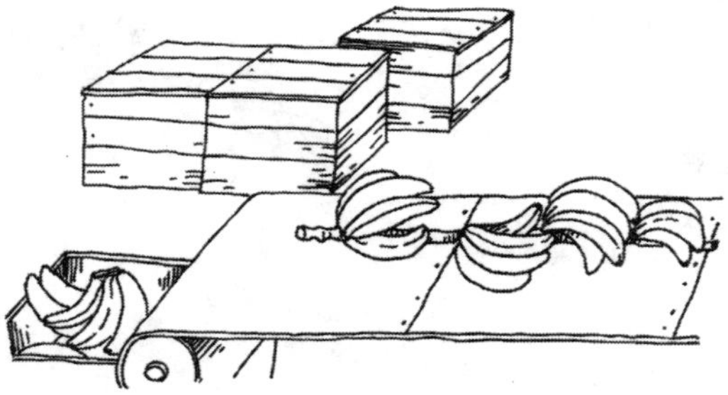

was   **were**

1. My sister _____ in the first grade.

spend   **spent**

2. I don't want to _____ all my money.

catch   **caught**

3. I _____ a fish when I went fishing.

drive   **drove**

4. My big sister will _____ us to the mall.

take   **took**

5. I will _____ my baby brother with me.

write   **wrote**

6. Yesterday, we _____ stories in school.

find   **found**

7. He helped me _____ my lost dog.

1. green plants make their own food

_____

2. green plants are the beginning of the food chain

_____

3. some animals eat plants

_____

4. some larger animals eat smaller animals

_____

5. these are all links in the food chain

_____

Goal 2, Standard 1/ESL Indicator: Edit written assignments to demonstrate knowledge of writing rules.

car   **food**

1. People grew their own _____ long ago.

corn   **dress**

2. They grew tomatoes and _____.

cows   **cats**

3. They milked the _____.

dolls   **ducks**

4. They raised chickens and _____.

don't   **eggs**

5. They ate the _____ from the chickens.

grew   **cow**

6. They _____ carrots and potatoes.

didn't   **farm**

7. The _____ was special.

Name

story

1. My sister read two _____ to me.

baby

2. There are a lot of _____ at the park.

grocery

3. We need to get _____ from the store.

family

4. There are five _____ on my street.

puppy

5. Did you see the _____ at the pet store?

city

6. We went to three _____ on our vacation.

Goal 1, Standard 3/ESL Indicator: Show appropriate use of new vocabulary, phrases, and structures by completing sentences with the plural of a given word.

shelter	food	television
toy		car

wants	needs

1. A house provides us with _____.

2. Our bodies need _____ for energy.

3. We like to watch _____.

4. A _____ store has many different kinds of toys.

5. My mom drives a _____ .

Goal 1, Standard 3/ESL Indicator: Show appropriate use of new vocabulary, phrases, and structures by completing sentences with given words.

Name

> farmer   police officer
>
> firefighter   doctor

_____   _____

_____   _____

Circle the begining letter of each word and identify the sound.

Goal 2, Standard 2/ESL Indicator: Recognize and write beginning letter sounds of words based on illustrations to demonstrate phonemic awareness.

	Mon.	Tues.	Wed.	Thurs.	Fri.	Sat.

100
90
80
70
60
50
40
30
20
10

1. How many shirts were made on Tuesday? __60__

2. How many shirts were made on Monday? __70__

3. How many more shirts were made on Wednesday than were made on Tuesday? __2 0__

4. How many more shirts were made on Friday than were made on Saturday? __10__

5. How many shirts in all were made on Wednesday, Thursday, and Friday? __220__

$$\begin{array}{r} 80 \\ +90 \\ +50 \\ \hline 220 \end{array}$$

6. How many shirts in all were made this week? __390__

$$\begin{array}{r} 70 \\ +60 \\ +80 \\ 490 \\ +50 \\ +40 \\ \hline 39 \end{array}$$

Name

> longer   shorter

1. is _____ than

2.  is _____ than

3. is _____ than

> bigger   smaller

4.  is _____ than

5. is _____ than

6. is _____ than

Goal 2, Standard 2/ESL Indicator: Compare and contrast the sizes of different objects based on illustrations.

Name _____

$25.50 $32.00 $12.00

$38.00 $22.25 $18.00

1. How much do the running shoes cost? $ 25.50

2. How much would it cost to buy the sandals and the running shoes? $43.50

$$\begin{array}{r} 18.00 \\ + 25.50 \\ \hline 43.50 \end{array}$$

3. How much more are the men's dress shoes than the bedroom slippers? $26.00

$$\begin{array}{r} 38.00 \\ - 12.00 \\ \hline 26.00 \end{array}$$

4. If you wanted two pairs of sandals, how much would you pay? $ 36.00

$$\begin{array}{r} 22.25 \\ + 22.25 \\ \hline 44.50 \end{array}$$

5. If you bought the two most expensive pairs of shoes, how much would you pay? $70.00

6. If you bought three pairs of running shoes, how much would you pay? $76.50

$$\begin{array}{r} 30 \\ + 32 \\ \hline 62 \end{array}$$

$$\begin{array}{r} 25.50 \\ + 25.50 \\ + 25.50 \\ \hline 75.50 \end{array}$$

Goal 2, Standard 2/ESL Indicator: Analyze and interpret data provided in an illustration to respond to written questions.

Name

harbor   **wave**

1. A _____ keeps ships safe from storms.

ship   **cargo**

2. A _____ ship carries goods from country to

country.

Cocoa   **Harbor**

3. _____ is made in Nigeria.

goods   **waves**

4. Storms can have big _____.

products   **harbors**

5. Countries buy _____ from each other.

Waves   **Goods**

6. _____ are products that are grown or made

in a country.

containers   **ships**

7. Goods are put in _____ on a ship.

Name

| square | triangle | circle | rectangle |

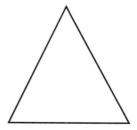

1. This shape is a _____.

2. This shape is a _____.

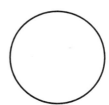

3. This shape is a _____.

4. This shape is a _____.

Goal 2, Standard 2/ESL Indicator: Identify shapes and use appropriate labels to complete sentences.

Name

1. How much does the camera cost? _____

2. How much would it cost to buy the computer and the answering machine? _____

3. How much more is the camcorder than the camera? _____

4. If you wanted two cameras, how much would you pay? _____

5. If you bought the two most expensive things in the store, how much would you pay? _____

6. How much more is the 19-inch TV than the 17-inch TV? _____

Name

1. How much does the ball cost? _____

2. How much does the doll and airplane cost

   altogether? _____

3. If the action figures were $4.99 and are now on sale for

   $2.99, how much would you save? _____

4. If you had $20.00 to spend and bought the ball, doll,

   and toy airplane, how much money would you have

   left? _____

Name

_____

_____

_____

_____

_____

_____

Name _____

1. I always _____

_____ .

2. I always _____

_____ .

3. I always _____

_____ .

4. I usually _____

_____ .

5. I usually _____

_____ .

6. I usually _____

_____ .

7. I never _____

_____ .

8. I never _____

_____ .

Goal 1, Standard 2/ESL Indicator: Express personal needs, feelings, and ideas in writing.

June						
Sunday	Monday	Tuesday	Wednesday	Thursday	Friday	Saturday
1	2	3	4	5	6	7
8	9	10	11	12	13	14
15	16	17	18	19	20	21
22	23	24	25	26	27	28
29	30					

1. June 23rd is a _Monday_.

2. June 10th is a _Tuesday_.

3. The Saturdays in June are the _7_, the _14_, the _21_, and the _28_.

4. The first day in June is a _Sunday_.

5. The last day in June is a _Monday_.

Goal 2, Standard 2/ESL Indicator: Record observations based on information provided through a calendar.

Name

have   **did**

1. Where _____did_____ you get those tomatoes?

buy   **bought**

2. She _____bought_____ a fish at the market.

had   **have**

3. We _____had_____ a good time yesterday.

want   **wanted**

4. He _____wanted_____ to buy some carrots.

catch   **caught**

5. The man _____caught_____ the fish in a river.

spend   **spent**

6. Mom _____spent_____ ten dollars at the market.

grow   **grew**

7. The farmer _____grew_____ the carrots on his farm.

Goal 1, Standard 3/ESL Indicator: Show appropriate use of new vocabulary, phrases, and structures by completing sentences with appropriate words.

There are all kinds of foods. You probably like some foods more than others. There are even some foods that you don't like at all.

Jason likes carrots, but he doesn't like beans. Nicolas likes tempura, but he doesn't like squash. Lupita likes chow mein, but she doesn't like pizza.

Most all of us have a favorite food. Carlos has a favorite food. It's sweet and sour pork. Pao's favorite food is black beans. Sara's favorite food is tempura. Maylee's favorite food is roast pork.

What about you? What do you like? What do you not like? What is your favorite food?

1. I like _pazpple_.

2. I do not like _beans_.

3. My favorite food is _pizza_.

4. Draw a picture of your favorite dinner in the box.

Name

July

Sunday	Monday	Tuesday	Wednesday	Thursday	Friday	Saturday
1	2	3	4	5	6	7
8	9	10	11	12	13	14
15	16	17	18	19	20	21
22	23	24	25	26	27	28
29	30	31				

1. How many days are there in the month of July? _31_

2. How many weeks are there in the month of July? _5_

3. How many Saturdays are there in July? _4_

4. How many days are in the first week of July? _5_

5. How many Sundays are there in July? _6_

6. How many days are in the last week of July? _3_

Goal 2, Standard 2/ESL Indicator: Record observations based on information obtained from a calendar.

pepper   **tomatoes**

1. You can buy ___pepper___ at a spice shop.

Swiss   **Egg**

2. ___Swiss___ cheese can be found in a cheese shop.

tea   **sausage**

3. A butcher shop has meats like ___sausage___ for sale.

ham   **mozzarella**

4. If you went to a cheese shop, you would find some

___mozzarella___

herb   **Swiss**

5. You can buy ___herb___ tea at a tea shop.

lamb   **bananas**

6. A fruit shop has ___bananas___ to sell.

Name

These are things I can do at home.

1. I can Watch Tv at home.
2. I can eat at
3. I can study.
4. I can play with toys
5. I can sleep at home.

This is a picture of what I like to do best when I'm at home.

Time Schedule				
Person Traveling	**Destination**	**Departure Time**	**Arrival Time**	**Method of Travel**
Jason	San Diego	11:30 A.M. *2 hrs*	1:30 P.M.	Bus
Pao	New York	2:30 P.M. *3 hrs*	5:30 P.M.	Plane
Nicolas	Arizona	7:00 A.M. *14 hrs.*	9:00 P.M.	Train
Maylee	San Francisco	7:30 A.M. *1 hr*	8:30 A.M.	Plane
Lupita & Carlos	Texas	8:00 A.M.	11:30 P.M.	Train & Bus

1. How many hours did it take Jason to travel to San Diego? _2 hours_

2. Where did Pao go? How many hours did it take?
New York 3 hours

3. Whose trip took the longest? _Nicolas and carlos_

4. Whose trip took the shortest? _Maylee_

 Look at the words with pictures in the **method of travel** section of the time schedule. Orally distinguish the vowel sounds of each of those words.

Goal 2, Standard 2/ESL Indicator: Distinguish vowel sounds of words presented through illustrations to demonstrate phonemic awareness.

Mars Shuttle			
Arrivals	**Gate**	**Departures**	**Gate**
7:30 A.M.	4	9:30 A.M.	5
9:00 A.M.	7	11:45 A.M.	8
1:15 P.M.	2	2:10 P.M.	6
4:00 P.M.	1	5:30 P.M.	3

1. At what time does the Mars shuttle depart from gate 3?

2. At what time does the Mars shuttle arrive at gate 7?

3. At what time does the Mars shuttle depart from gate 8?

4. At what time does the Mars shuttle arrive at gate 2?

Goal 2, Standard 2/ESL Indicator: Analyze and associate information presented in a chart to record time.

Name

cities   neighbors

1. People who live close to each other are *neighbors*

neighborhood   suburb

2. A *suburb* is a community close to a city.

city   town

3. A *town* is a small city.

community   village

4. A city is a large *community* where many people live and work.

5. I live in the state of *California*

6. I live in a *city* called *Fremont*

Write a sentence that tells about your neighborhood.

My t have friends in my neighborhood. I have a yard. Every body had colorful flowers and roses in my neighborhood.

Goal 1, Standard 3/ESL Indicator: Show appropriate use of new vocabulary, phrases, and structures by completing sentences with appropriate words.

Name

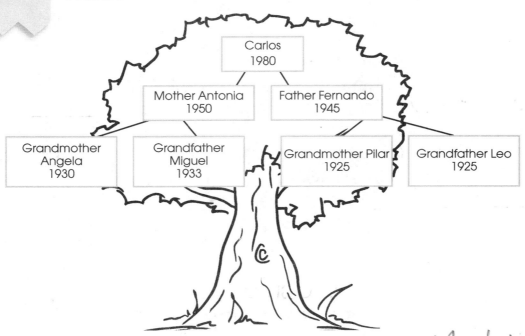

Carlos
1980

Mother Antonia
1950

Father Fernando
1945

Grandmother Angela
1930

Grandfather Miguel
1933

Grandmother Pilar
1925

Grandfather Leo
1925

1. What are the names of Carlos' parents? _Mother Antonia Father Fereando._

2. Grandmother Angela and Grandfather Miguel are the parents of _Mother Antonia_

3. Grandfather Leo's son is _Father Fernando_

4. What year was Carlos born? _1980_.

Following the teacher's directions, write a sentence about your family. Then draw a line under the nouns and a ring around the words.

I have four people in my family. I have a father a mother and a sister.

Goal 1, Standard 3/ESL Indicator: Show appropriate use of new vocabulary, phrases, and structures by following teacher s directions to complete sentences.

pottery   **small**

1. Carlos's mother has a store that sells ___*pottery*___

came   **imports**

2. She ___*imports*___ the pottery from Mexico.

state   **town**

3. The pottery is made in a small ___*town*___ in Mexico.

sells   **buys**

4. She ___*sells*___ the pottery to people in the U.S.

grandparents   **ancestors**

5. Carlos's mother buys the pottery from her

___*grandparents*___ in Mexico.

Write two sentences about a store you might like to have.

*I want to e a sto I want
to be cause they sell
food. We get to*

Name

Mexico   **England**

1. Sara's family came to the U.S. from __Mexico__.

Tennessee   **California**

2. They settled in a small farm community in __California__.

Texas   **Kansas**

3. Then they moved to __Texas__.

fast car   **covered wagon**

4. They traveled in a __fast__ __car__.

miles   **days**

5. They had to travel 615 __miles__.

Write two sentences about where your family or a family you know came from.

__My family came from__
__India. They came looking for__
__a Job.__

Name

Hong Kong	Chinese junk	harbor
fisherman	markets	language
Cantonese	children	

Goal 2, Standard 2/ESL Indicator: Consult print and non-print resources to obtain information to complete a task.

ancestors   sister

1. Our _____ances_____ came from many countries to the United States.

walked   traveled

2. They _____ by plane, train, bus, ship, and car.

states   cities

3. The United States is made up of 50 _____.

state   nation

4. The United States is a _____.

EXTENSION ACTIVITY Using two of the vocabulary words, compose a sentence with each one.

1. _____

_____

2. _____

_____

stripes   stars

1. The U.S. flag has 13 ___*Stripes*___.

stars   citzens

2. The U.S. flag has 50 ___*Stars*___.

symbol   cities

3. Each star stands for a state, thus each star is

a ___*Symbol*___ representing each state.

Write a sentence about the United States flag.

The colors of the united statesare flag

white, red, and blue

Name

United States

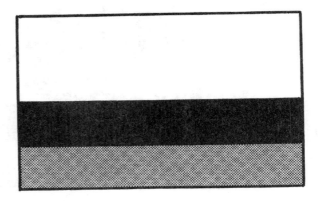

Colombia

Mexico

China

Write sentences that describe two of the four flags.

1. The united states flag has 50 stars Eedh repleasing State.

2. But the China flag has 1 big star and 4 small stars.

Goal 2, Standard 2/ESL Indicator: Identify and associate pictures of flags with the names of countries to demonstrate knowledge.

Name

border	states	near

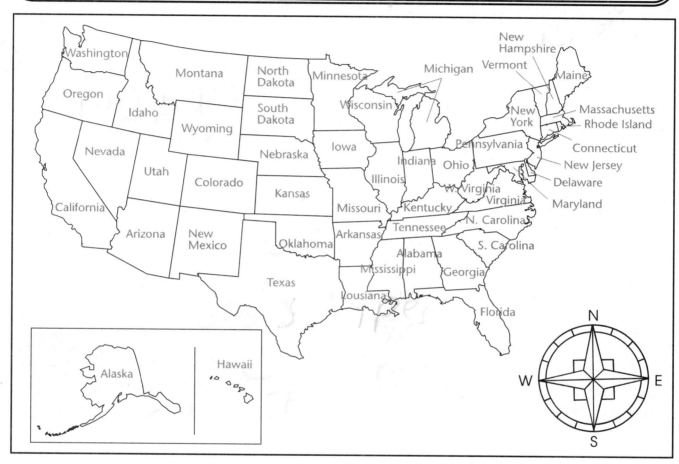

1. Color the state where you live red.

2. Color the states that are your neighbors blue.

3. The United States is composed of 50 _____.

4. California and Nevada _____ each other.

5. New York and New Hampshire are _____.

6. What state is west of your state? _____

Goal 2, Standard 2/ESL Indicator: Recognize directional words on a map and respond to questions in writing to demonstrate comprehension.

Name _____

laws   helps

1. A good citizen obeys the _____.

obey   protect

2. Laws are made to _____ citizens.

environment   tops

3. A good citizen helps to protect the _____.

school   outside

4. Good citizens help others in their _____ and community.

On the lines below, write what you think it means to be a good citizen.

_____

_____

_____

_____